A QUICK GUIDE TO

Reaching Struggling Writers

K–5

Other Books in the Workshop Help Desk Series

A Quick Guide to
Teaching Persuasive Writing, K–2
SARAH PICARD TAYLOR

A Quick Guide to
Boosting English Acquisition in Choice Time, K–2
ALISON PORCELLI AND CHERYL TYLER

A Quick Guide to
Making Your Teaching Stick, K–5
SHANNA SCHWARTZ

For more information about these and other titles,
visit www.heinemann.com.

A QUICK GUIDE TO
Reaching Struggling Writers
K–5

M. COLLEEN CRUZ

Workshop Help Desk Series
Edited by Lucy Calkins
with the Teachers College Reading and Writing Project

HEINEMANN
Portsmouth, NH

Heinemann
361 Hanover Street
Portsmouth, NH 03801–3912
www.heinemann.com

Offices and agents throughout the world

Library of Congress Cataloging-in-Publication Data

Cruz, Maria Colleen.
  A quick guide to reaching struggling writers, K–5 / M. Colleen Cruz.
      p. cm. — (Workshop help desk series)
  Includes bibliographical references.
  ISBN 13: 978-0-325-02595-7
  ISBN 10: 0-325-02595-9
  1. English language—Composition and exercises—Study and teaching
(Elementary). 2. Language arts—Remedial teaching. I. Title.
  LB1576.C845 2008
  372.62′3—dc22   2008027292

SERIES EDITOR: *Lucy Calkins and the Teachers College Reading and Writing Project*
EDITOR: *Kate Montgomery*
PRODUCTION: *Elizabeth Valway*
COVER DESIGN: *Jenny Jensen Greenleaf*
COVER PHOTO: *Peter Cunningham*
INTERIOR DESIGN: *Jenny Jensen Greenleaf*
COMPOSITION: *House of Equations, Inc.*
MANUFACTURING: *Steve Bernier*

Printed in the United States of America on acid-free paper
22 21 20 19 GP 9 10 11

For P.S. 54

CONTENTS

ACKNOWLEDGMENTS ix

INTRODUCTION xi

1 "I'm not a good writer." 1

2 "My hand hurts." 17

3 "I don't know how to spell." 30

4 "I don't have anything to write about." 43

5 "I never get to write anything I want to write." 59

6 "I'm done." 69

WORKS CITED 80

BOOKS RECOMMENDED BY THIS AUTHOR
(available on our website, www.firsthand.heinemann.com)

ACKNOWLEDGMENTS

I'd like to thank a whole lot of people for helping me get this book together. First, I want to thank Lucy Calkins for being a visionary mentor by helping me see that the topic of struggling writers was not something I should just study on my own, but rather something I should make a central part of my work as an educator. I'd also like to thank Kathleen Tolan, who was my first staff developer and one of the first people to help me differentiate my instruction. I also owe much gratitude to all my colleagues at the Teachers College Reading and Writing Project who helped me bounce ideas around and continue to challenge me, especially Maggie Beattie, Mary Ehrenworth, Shana Frazin, Cory Gillette, Amanda Hartman, Christine Holley, Beth Neville, Laurie Pessah, Sarah Picard Taylor, Kate Roberts, Rob Ross, Jen Serravallo, and Emily Smith. I am very grateful to my Heinemann editor, Kate Montgomery, who yet again went way beyond the call of duty. I'd also like to thank the Heinemann production staff, especially, Jillian Scahill, Elizabeth Tripp, and Elizabeth Valway. Thank you also to the teachers, coaches, administrators, and students at the schools where I did much of the piloting of the work in this book, including P.S. 18, P.S. 29, P.S. 54, P.S. 58, P.S. 94, P.S. 180, P.S. 321, and P.S. 503. In particular, Peggy Halford from P.S. 58 was immeasurably helpful. Much thanks to the writers in my writing group—especially Kristen Beers, Sarah Colmaire, Theresa

Luogo, Priya Manocha, Kathleen Estes Milano, and Barbara Pinto—as well as all the teachers in my specialty group. Thank you to my family for putting up with yet another distraction. And finally, thank you, Nadine—you know why.

Frustration All Around

K ids get stuck all the time while writing. Truthfully, we do, too. This book is not about those temporary sputters and stalls that happen to all of us. This book is about those students who are stuck all the time. Students we frequently see sitting for several minutes, sometimes the whole class period, with nary a word scratched upon the page. Students whose notebooks we flip through hopefully, only to find oodles of blank pages hidden between a few written-upon ones. Students who suddenly have to go to the bathroom, sharpen their pencils, or visit the nurse every time writing is on the agenda. Mild-mannered students who suddenly start cracking jokes and talking back. Tough ones who burst into tears.

This book is intended to help those of us who have students in our classrooms who don't write.

In other words, this book is for every teacher who has a writing workshop.

We all know that no two students are alike. So it stands to reason that no two struggling students will need exactly the same kind of teaching.

Before we explore what each student comes to us knowing and believing about writing, we must first try to leave all of our misconceptions at the proverbial door. It is only then that we can best find the right strategies that will fit each student.

There are, of course, as many different kinds of struggles as there are faces of students. However, for the purposes of this book, I have explored the six most common things students say to us while shooting up the flare to let us know they are in trouble:

"I'm not a good writer."
"My hand hurts."
"I don't know how to spell."
"I don't have anything to write about."
"I never get to write anything I want to write."
"I'm done."

Some students may never have said these things, but you can almost see the thought bubbles above their heads. Some students' struggles fit into more than one category. Some students' struggles fall firmly into one. You will also notice that sometimes one struggle can affect another.

My hope is that you will flip directly to the chapters that address the struggles most urgently uttered in your classroom right now. Each chapter is organized into three major sections meant to be of practical help right away:

▶ researching in order to understand what's going on with the student

- choosing strategies we can put into action
- planning for next steps

The work in this book comes from my experiences as a classroom teacher in New York City, working with both general education and special education populations. The students discussed in this book are composites created from the hundreds of students I've worked with and learned from over the years. My rehearsal for this book has spanned years and has included not only the days I spent teaching but also the evenings I spent torturing myself over a garbled notebook or over the realization that the student I'd dismissed the day before had been pleading for help.

I've also culled a bulk of these ideas from my current colleagues at the Teachers College Reading and Writing Project, where I work as a literacy consultant in New York City schools and across the country. Lucy Calkins, the founding director of the Project, in addition to being one of my primary mentors, was instrumental in pushing me to think and rethink my ideas about how to best help *all* students learn to write better. My other main influences for this book were Mel Levine, Donald Graves, Katie Wood Ray, Carl Anderson, Lev Vygotsky, and Katherine Bomer. Countless teachers, administrators, service providers, and students have offered up suggestions, crystallized my thinking, and challenged me in ways that you will see over and over again in the pages of this book.

It is also worth noting that I am working from the assumption that you either have a writing workshop up and going in your classroom or plan to have one very soon. I am assuming that you teach your students writing on a daily basis. You teach students to think of writing as a process, and your students have choice of topics, voice, and sometimes of structure in their writing. You teach units across the year that focus on process and genre—for example, one unit might invite students to write poetry and another might spotlight revision. Writing workshop is the teaching method I was raised in and immersed in since I first entered this profession and I embrace it in the book. It is challenging for me to think outside of its boundaries. That said, even if you do not have a writing workshop, with a little interpretation, you will probably find that many of the strategies I propose in this book will work for your classroom as well.

CHAPTER ONE

"I'm not a good writer."

I know them when I see them.

Sometimes they groan when writing time is announced.

Sometimes they ask for the bathroom pass, or to sharpen their pencils, or to see the nurse.

Sometimes they carve holes in their writing notebooks with the points of their pens. Or else they erase until there is nothing left but desktop.

Or they pull their hoodies up over their heads and lay their heads down on their arms, looking for all the world like they are trying to become invisible.

They don't have to say anything at all. But, if I happen to ask what's going on, and they happen to feel safe that day, they might say, "I'm not a good writer."

We strive to create classrooms where all of our students and their different learning styles are honored. We know that not every student is going to be naturally good at math or science or even art. And yet, for some reason, when a student feels she is not a good writer, many of us take it personally. We love writing. Or maybe *we* don't love writing, but we feel for some reason that our students should love writing. And besides, there are so many other kids in the class who maybe aren't the most sophisticated writers yet are proud of their work nonetheless. "I want to share," they'll say. "Wanna read my piece?" they'll ask.

And so we feel helpless when faced with a student who does not exude that same confidence, who doesn't see himself as a good writer. Or perhaps we feel guilty because we've been teaching day after day, week after week, without noticing that we're not quite reaching every single student after all. Of course, even if we have noticed these students—perhaps even obsessed about them—they still can make us feel guilty. We've noticed and worried about them, but have we helped? Sometimes, because none of the methods in the books we read seem to work with those kids, we end up doing nothing beyond worrying.

I know I certainly felt that way as I raced between my thirty-two fourth graders. I would see them—I always saw them. And I wanted to help them. But since I didn't always know what to do, I sometimes simply walked past them, hoping I would figure something out later to help them. And sometimes I did. I talked to the wise colleague or went to the perfectly timed workshop, and I was able to return fully prepared to help those students. But often I simply worried about them and tried to smile at them while moving quickly on to students I knew how to help.

Nowadays, I still smile at these students. They are the ones I make a beeline for whenever I step into a classroom. They are the ones I revel in and can't wait to pull a seat next to so I can get to know them better. Because helping these students grow has become one of the fundamental reasons I am still a teacher—and I've now embarked on a lifelong journey to discover ways to teach them.

Understanding Our Students' Writing Identities

Mel Levine says that childhood is one of the few times in our lives when we have to do things that we are not good at. School is wrought with hurdles and obstacles for students who struggle academically. It is also filled with opportunities for students to find their affinities.

As adults, if we are not good at something, we avoid it. And if we can't avoid it, we develop strategies for dealing with it—we use calculators when we're bad at arithmetic; we call a tech support line when the computer is on the fritz.

Unfortunately, our students cannot avoid the demands of school that they feel no affinity for, no matter how much they shrink into their hoodies. Writing is one of those demands.

We can begin to help these students if we don't let them shrink so far into those hoodies that we stop seeing them. We need to see them, and to see them as writers. You can start helping these students if you take a few minutes away from conferring during one writing period to just observe a student who has been off your radar. Notice the student's behaviors: her posture, her focus on the paper, where her eyes look in the classroom:

- Does she look to the chart you made during the minilesson?

- Does she ask someone sitting at her table for help?

- Does she spend a long time writing the date at the top of the page or otherwise make herself look busy?

- Does the student spend most of her writing time drawing?

- Does she intentionally make it known to her classmates that she is not writing today?

All of these things can give us insight into how the student views herself in relation to writing. We can tell whether the student uses any independent strategies to get herself going, such as rereading charts or checking at past writing. We might notice that she tries to make herself busy, perhaps because she is trying to present the image of a student who has it all together. We might even see that she is quite resourceful at getting classmates to help her out of a jam, showing strength in social skills (or overreliance on them).

It can help to follow up this work by taking some time to study that student's writing work for insights into the student's writing identity. To get a fuller picture of the student, look at her writing across several curriculum areas. Then you might look to see if there are any places where her confidence seems markedly stronger or markedly weaker. A few key questions come to mind when determining writer confidence:

- Are there some subjects about which the student writes more or with more confidence than others?

▌ Are there any places where she gives insights into her feelings about writing?

▌ Does it appear that the student writes with more confidence when the writing is more open-ended or when the writing is more prescribed?

By looking at student work, we might see that some students sputter during writing workshop, but when writing about a recent science experiment, their pens seem never to stop. That could indicate that the students may not struggle with stringing words together into sentences in instances when they are confident about the content, but when the content is a little tougher (which can be the case when students are trying to write a personal narrative on a topic that makes them feel vulnerable), the students' confidence takes a nosedive. Or perhaps, as was the case for quite a few of my students, we find that in their notebooks, students will actually have written brief rants about writing—and those rants express exactly what they find so daunting. "My hand hurts! I can't think of what to write! I hate writing!" an entry might read. We might also discover that the student is perhaps more comfortable with fill-in-the-blank or very controlled writing. In those instances, we need to do a little digging to learn whether the student's comfort zones reflect her past schooling experiences or whether they are more indicative of a fear of making a mistake.

Once we have gotten a better sense of a student's behaviors during writing time, and have spent time studying her work, we might then make a plan to interview the student. This interview is not the same sort of conversation we might have when researching what to teach in a conference. Instead, we are working to get as full a picture as possible of this student's sense of self, and we particularly want to gain insights that will help us make bridges to writing.

For some students, this conversation will take place during a regular writing workshop; for other students, we'll set aside a different time to have the conversation. Either way, we'll make it very clear to the student that we want to learn a little more about her and that this is in no way a punitive conversation. The tone should be one of respectful interest.

Following are some things we might want to find out about the student:

- What does the student enjoy doing when she's not in school?
- What does the student enjoy in school?
- How does the student feel about writing?
- What is the student's favorite piece that she's written this year?
- What is her least favorite piece?
- What does the student find hard about writing?
- What does the student find easy about writing?

From this conversation, we should discover even more about the student that can help us create writing situations and teaching points perfectly tailored to her strengths and passions. We can discover perhaps that the student is a ballet dancer on the weekends. Perhaps the piece of writing that we thought of as the student's best was not what the student chose. We should also have a sense of what the student thinks matters about writing when she tells us what she finds easy and what she finds hard.

After observing the student, having a conversation, looking at her writing, and perhaps checking in with last year's teacher, we should have a good picture of who this student is as a writer, and probably an even stronger sense of the student as a person. We are now on the track to helping this student develop a more positive writing identity. In order to do that, we can create a plan of action. The plan of action might be based on the following:

- the student's strengths, both writing and nonwriting
- the student's interests
- the student's struggles
- the student's view of self

The plan of action should address the writer as a whole—and most certainly begin by working with the student's areas of strength in mind.

Strategies for Helping Students Develop Stronger Writing Identities

When we think about students slamming down their notebooks, tearing up their pages, or asking repeatedly to go to the bathroom during writing time, it can be disheartening. It helps to keep in mind that there is a lot we can do to help them, once we've gotten to know them better as people and as writers. We can then begin the work that could take one class period, but more likely a few weeks or months—the quest to help a student become a confident writer. We can do this by exploring every area of our classroom lives, from the ways our students interact with each other to the lessons we choose to teach to individual students.

Create a Community of Writers Who Struggle and Succeed Together

At the start of the school year, each of us works to create a community in our classroom. We play name games, try trust activities, and share personal stories. As part of this, we share stories of writing struggles and successes. It is crucial to continue building and renewing the community all year long.

There are many ways I've seen this work done in the classrooms I know best. Some teachers make a special share time on Fridays, when students and their teacher sit in a circle and share, popcorn style, a story of their writing that week. The teacher often jumps in to share an incident in which she struggled as a writer or made a breakthrough as a writer. Then one child, then another and another share similar stories. In some classrooms, this sharing of writing-life stories happens between partners, when teachers suggest that instead of sharing actual pieces of writing, partners talk about moments of despair, insight, or discovery.

One teacher told me that companionable talk between writers seemed so essential to her that she wanted this to be a resource for children at the point of need, yet she worried that allowing children to share writing-life stories might invite constant talk during every writing workshop. She couldn't stomach the idea of a writing workshop filled with chatter. So that teacher created a special student conference table complete with pens, sticky notes, and an egg timer. When a student wanted company as a writer—perhaps when she did something particularly fabulous or when she felt especially paralyzed—she could simply tap her partner's shoulder, walk over to the conference table with her partner, set the egg timer, and have a short conversation.

Creating opportunities like these in our classrooms benefits the entire class, strengthening everyone's sense of community. That said, probably no one benefits more than the student who does not view himself as a good writer. He will soon see that he is not the only one who struggles with writing. And, perhaps more importantly, he will see that there are ways to overcome writing difficulties.

Think Vygotsky: Teach into the Zone of Proximal Development

Lev Vygotsky taught us that a child learns best when she is challenged within her zone of proximal development. When a child finds a task too easy, she is not learning anything and might in fact become bored and see learning as not for her. If a challenge is too much for a child, she will become frustrated and unable to learn and she will begin to think learning is not for her. The challenge for educators is to strike that fine balance of creating opportunities where the child feels both challenged and supported. When considering our work in writing, we can ensure that students have many opportunities to build on their areas of strength while reaching for the next goal.

So, for a child who struggles to fill up the page, or even write beyond a sentence or two, we don't say, "Everyone must produce a two-page piece." That would just set the child up for frustration. Alternatively, we don't just accept the one sentence as the best the child can do. Instead, we might have a conference with the student, where we talk about setting goals for ourselves that stretch us past our own best work. And together, with the child, we set a goal that the student can meet during the day's session, say five lines one day, eight lines the next, knowing we will build on it in the immediate future.

When we consistently teach in this way, considering a student's zone of proximal development, and the student finds himself more and more capable of rising to greater and greater challenges without being overwhelmed by frustration-level demands, the student's confidence level will undoubtedly rise.

Consider a Student's Affinities

Fortunately, writing is made up of a variety of genres, topics, and forms. So many, in fact, that for even the most reluctant writer, with a little bit of digging, we can often find some sort of connection to that student's areas of passionate interest. In my first year of teaching, I longed for read-aloud every day. It was something I felt good about and the kids seemed to enjoy. Every day I would get better and better at read-aloud.

And eventually I began to steal ideas from read-aloud to transfer into the subject areas I didn't feel so confident about. I realized my students were really well behaved when sitting on the rug. So I changed my students' spots for math from tables to the rug.

If a student who is declaring himself a bad writer was very successful writing informational books, we might look to the unit we are currently teaching, say fiction, and consider how we can build a bridge for that child. We might say, "One thing I know about writers is that they can often really get going when they reflect on what they did well in the past. I noticed that when we were working on informational books, you were on fire. What were some of the topics that you wrote about? Maybe we can think about how to turn those into ideas for fiction stories." When we work like this with a child, we are taking an area a student already feels confident about and using it, much like I used read-aloud, to explore areas where he has less confidence.

Additionally, after interviewing a student and making sure that the classroom offers plenty of opportunities for him to succeed outside of writing time, it's important to build on those feelings of success by finding similar affinities, or areas of expertise in writing, specifically.

These areas do not have to be big, like a talent for personal narrative, although they could be. More often than not, we'll discover that a student has the market cornered on something more surprising and probably more practical for the average elementary school colleague. I make it my job to uncover an area of writing I can not only cultivate in this student but also announce to the whole class, saying that this student is the go-to person for this particular area of expertise. In my fourth-grade classroom, which I wrote about in *Independent Writing* (2004), I created a "Help Wanted— Help Offered" bulletin board. Students would post their strengths, such as "I'm a good speller," as well as the help they needed, such as "Does anyone have any good ideas for an 'About the Author' page?"

Partner the Student with a Younger Writing Buddy

You might have noticed in your interview and observation of the student that she talked with pride about caring for a little brother, sister, or cousin. Or maybe you just noticed that she lights up whenever she works with someone who seems to need her. This student might be the perfect person to pair with a writing buddy from a lower grade. In fact, you might decide in the end that you want to create a long-term relationship with one of the lower grades, meeting on a regular basis to share writing, offer tips, and celebrate.

Often students who feel like they are not good writers simply need to see someone else who is struggling, someone else who needs reassurance. It's amazing how many students who just minutes before were despairing that their writing was terrible will compliment and coo over a younger student whose own writing is at a much lower level developmentally. It's also true that often the frequent and admiring eyes of this younger student can do much more to build the confidence of a self-conscious writer than all of our efforts combined.

Use That Student's Writing as an Exemplar in the Classroom

Many of us use student models for everything from classroom management ("Thank you for showing me you're ready to work, Malcolm") to teaching alternative math algorithms ("Can everyone look up here and see the new addition strategy that Christina is going to teach us?").

During writing workshop, we can make sure we are always on the lookout to be impressed by each of our students, especially those students who do not feel so very impressive. We note each independently used strategy, each new idea, each word choice as another opportunity to share this student's best work with his colleagues. The challenging part is to find something that the student is taking a risk to do, not just something he already knows he does well.

If Christina has been using dialogue effectively in her stories since September, it will not inspire Christina or her classmates to point out that she uses dialogue in her stories. However, if Christina has tried something new, such as using some flashy punctuation or pulling out her mentor text to look for possible ways to craft an ending, we should stop the presses and make an announcement. The announcement should be given in a tone of *I'm not surprised* mixed with the energy of a discovery: *I plan to use this strategy myself right away.*

This method works best when you have a classroom that very much works as a community and follows the teacher's cues. This strategy can also backfire if either the students are unwilling to view each other with new eyes or the student you are highlighting does not believe you are sincere.

Teach Students About the Struggles and Successes of Various Published Writers

I feel the reason so many Americans enjoy reading *People* and *Us Weekly* is not just to see what not to wear or who wore it better, although that's part of it. I think the main reason we enjoy (or hate) these magazines is because they hold up celebrities and their lives as examples for us to scrutinize. If that star is having trouble losing the baby weight, then I shouldn't feel so bad. If this star can overcome his fear of flying, then I can, too. We compare and contrast ourselves with these stars and their successes and failures all the time.

Writers are just such stars to our students. We can take advantage of this by collecting stories of writers' own struggles and successes. We can trawl the Internet, looking for authors' web pages, and collect those stories. We can read books about writers' lives to our students, such as Paula Graham's *Speaking of Journals* (1999) and Paul Janeczko's *Seeing the Blue Between* (2006). We can pore over the back flaps of book covers to try to glean what the writer's process might be. We can invite writers to our schools and ask them to talk about the challenges of writing as well as the joys.

We can then collect all the quotes, tips, and ideas we find and cocreate a living bulletin board that we add to and find inspiration from all year long. Quotes such as this one from Kate DiCamillo: "I write two pages a day. Usually, those two pages stink pretty bad. I rewrite. And rewrite. And rewrite. And rewrite. And rewrite. And each time I rewrite, the pages get a little better." Or Jon Scieszka, who describes writing as hard labor, like "ditch-digging." Or read from Jacqueline Woodson's website, where she describes writing as hard work and says,

"Revising is hard. Thinking of new things to write about is hard. And difficulty makes it that much more rewarding."

When we do this *People* magazine–type work, students who think they are not good writers and that writing is hard will realize not only that they are not alone in feeling this way but that "real" writers—ones they admire and whose books they read—feel this way sometimes, too. We all do at one time in our lives or another. We can help make that knowledge as well as make the rewards of persevering public.

Your Reflections

I'm imagining that you've run into a few students who disappear into their hoodies or spend their writing time looking as if they are praying no one will ever read what they have written.

Take a couple of minutes to jot down the names of the students in your class whom you have heard say, "I'm not a good writer."

Then jot down your plans for next steps in working with each of these students. Have you already interviewed and observed the student or do you still need to do that? Do you already have some of the strategies mentioned in place in your classroom? Are there ones you want to try?

I am reminded of Rosa, one of my former students, who moaned for the first month of school, whenever we had writing time. She would use her arm and hair to cover up her writing as she went. "I'm a terrible writer. A terrible writer," she would say, shaking her head whenever I asked to see her work. She didn't put spaces between her words, her letters were cramped together, and her spelling was almost entirely phonetic. But, when I asked Rosa to read aloud her work to me, which was influenced mostly by the heavy diet of fantasy books that she read, I was bowled over. And I told her so. I spent much of the year working on helping her see just what a truly fantastic writer she was. She was a perfect student for the strategies discussed in this chapter as well as the next.

CHAPTER TWO

"My hand hurts."

I was this kid. Actually, I still am this kid. My favorite way to draft and write long chunks of text is on the computer. Whenever I have to write longhand, my hand starts to cramp, my handwriting gets progressively harder to read, and I develop a dark red splotch on the first knuckle of my middle finger.

When I was a child, I used to sit at the dining room table, where I was supposed to be doing my homework, and stall. I wanted to write. I always had tons of ideas. But my hand literally hurt. It hurt to the point that I actually developed a callus on that knuckle on my middle finger. When I was younger, I would cry. As I grew older and crying was no longer an acceptable reaction to homework, I began to avoid anything that had to do with putting a pencil in my hand for an extended period of time.

This is unfortunately a place where many of our students end up. The physical struggles with writing making it all but impossible to move on to the work of developing ideas, crafting sentences, and creating whole stories and essays that move readers.

Understanding Students Who Are Struggling with the Manual Work of Writing

In a way, we're actually lucky when a student tells us his hand hurts. He is giving us an insight into a fairly straightforward issue without our doing much digging. However, I have heard teachers absentmindedly say, when a student complains about his hurting hand, to just "shake it off," or perhaps the teacher doesn't say anything to the student at all, but privately thinks of the student as lazy or just trying to avoid writing. I have certainly said and thought all of those things.

After all, how *can* we tell when something is actually wrong and the student is not just using the hurting-hand complaint as a stalling strategy? Not to mention that we know that as the student moves through the grades, greater and greater levels of stamina are going to be asked of him. What are we to do—simply let a student whose hand hurts off the proverbial writing hook?

Well, first things first. We need to remember that whenever a student is not writing, there is something we can actively do to help. The chances are good that even if the student is not putting the most accurate words around the problem, there is in fact a problem. Children have that fundamental desire to learn. The tricky thing with "My hand hurts" is that sometimes it is just a misnomer. There might be something else going on that the student might not be consciously aware of—weak self-confidence, writer's block, or fear of spelling something incorrectly, for instance. So, one of the first things we need to do is to research a little bit to see whether or not the student actually needs help with the physical aspects of writing.

First, we should observe the student while in the act of writing (which, depending on the severity of the avoidance, might be a feat unto itself). Some things you might want to look for include insights into posture and pencil grip:

▸ Does the student sit relaxed and upright? Or does the student slouch, huddle, or seem to be exceedingly tense?

▸ Are the table and chair the correct height? Does the student's feet touch the floor? Is the table two inches above the bend of the elbow?

▸ Does the student's wrist extend across the paper in a natural and relaxed way? Or does it bend like a hook?

▸ Does the student hold her fingers in the recommended tripod grip, with the thumb, pointer, and middle finger forming a triangle that is supported by the ring and pinkie fingers? Or do you see another grip such as the thumb crossing the other two fingers? Or is she holding the pencil in a fist or tucking it between the pointer and the ring fingers or some other nontripod grip?

▸ Are there times of the day when the student's writing seems more facile than others? First thing in the morning? After gym or playtime?

You also might find more information by looking at the student's writing, either in a notebook or on paper. This could give you insights into the kind of pressure the student is exerting on the pencil as well as any other patterns of success or frustration. You might consider these questions:

- ▶ Can you feel the texture of the writing through the other side of the paper?

- ▶ Do you notice places where the pencil has broken or gone through the paper?

- ▶ Do you see that there are times of the day when the student writes more or less? Are there certain genres or topics the student has more writing volume around? Or is there a fairly consistent pattern in terms of number of lines written?

- ▶ Do you notice cramped handwriting or handwriting that is in other ways difficult to read?

All of these pieces of observational research can give us some insights into how we can best angle a conversation with the student. If the student has told us his hand hurts, we might simply ask if he has any idea as to why. He might not know why, but his response will help give us a lever when we offer strategies later on.

If the student has not directly said that his hand hurts but we have observed some of the behaviors listed earlier, including occasional hand rubbing and perhaps a parent note or two saying that the student has difficulty with the volume of writing you expect, you might want to ask the student what he finds hard about writing (only after having asked what he finds easy, of course). If the student offers an indication that some of the trouble might be connected to the physical aspects of writing, then you might consider some of the following strategies.

Strategies for Helping Students Who Struggle with the Physical Work of Writing

Certainly the first move you'll want to make is to touch base with the occupational therapist in your building if you are fortunate enough to have one. Not necessarily to refer the child for services, although you might choose to do that, but rather to get the therapist's latest, best thinking about how to support a child who is finding writing challenging. For example, when I was originally beginning work on this book, I thought the only thing I needed to concern myself with was the actual act of putting pen to paper when thinking about the physical aspects of writing. It was Peggy Halford, an occupational therapist, who taught me that there is a direct correlation between the amount of stamina a student has and her ability to wield a pencil easily and well, regardless of whether or not she requires occupational therapy services.

Additionally, if the child is receiving services, you might discover that there are simple modifications and strategies that the occupational therapist has already introduced to the student that you can reinforce in the classroom setting, giving the student an additional layer of support.

If, however, you do not have access to an occupational therapist and you already have some information on the patterns you are seeing in the student's writing, you might want to try some basic strategies I have learned from various occupational therapists. Clearly nothing can replace the expertise of these trained professionals, and some of the strategies they use are very challenging or just not feasible in a workshop classroom environment. The following strategies are the easiest to implement as well as the most effective within writing workshop.

For Students Who Seem to Struggle with Writing Stamina

You might have noticed while researching that certain students wrote volumes no matter what time of day, what the topic was, or what the genre was. You probably noticed other students who wrote the most during the morning or after physical education class. As I mentioned earlier, there is a direct correlation between stamina and students' ability to keep up with the physical rigors of writing. Many of your students, and especially those who struggle from physical demands during particular times of the day, may benefit from the following:

▶ Schedule writing workshop in the morning if you can. Because of the amount of effort writing takes from all parts of the brain, many teachers find that writing in the morning while the students are still fresh can go a long way toward increasing stamina.

▶ Offer whole-body warm-ups before writing time. Some teachers have students do jumping jacks. Others play a rousing game of Simon Says. Getting the blood moving and the gross muscle groups woken up can help students focus more closely on fine-motor tasks like writing. These activities can also be used as breaks during an extended writing session.

▶ Provide a time limit for writing time and teach students how to pace themselves. Some students use all their energy in the first several minutes of writing time and then spend the rest of the session wondering how much time they have left. Some teachers let their students know that they will have fifteen minutes to work before taking a break to talk to their partner. Then they have the students write for another fifteen minutes before the teaching share. Some teachers use clocks that give clear visual clues as to how much time the students have left, such as the Time Timer, which gradually removes a red film from the minutes so that students can get a sense of the time they have left by simply looking at how much red is left on the clock.

▶ Practice quickwrites, where students write as quickly as possible for a set amount of time—anywhere from one to five minutes. The students have a goal of writing nonstop without lifting their pens. Some teachers encourage students to try this within a particular genre the class is studying. Other teachers have students try this as a stream-of-consciousness type of writing, complete with students jotting down "I'm stuck" rather than stopping writing. Doing this exercise on a regular basis can help students see just how much they are capable of writing, while also helping them improve their writing fluency.

▶ Model stamina goal setting in writing. Frequently begin writing sessions by asking students to set a stamina goal for themselves. I like to have students create a little box at the top of the page where they write their personal goal. They might decide to write for a certain number of minutes without stopping or else to try to reach a pre-determined stopping point—perhaps designated with a star. Other students set up word-count goals, where they try to increase their word count each day they sit down to write. The goals are set up so the student is competing only against his personal best, not a predetermined number of pages or other goal set by us.

For Students Who Struggle with Pencil Grip and Posture

Children in grades K–2 are the perfect age to work on adjusting their grip and posture. Here are some things you might decide to incorporate into your classroom for all of your students:

▶ *Handwriting practice every day.* This is not meant to take the place of writing workshop, or even to take up too much time. In fact, many occupational therapists believe that students should have intensive practice for only five minutes a day, using proper posture, pencil grip, and letter formation. Some schools opt to use a commercial program such as Handwriting Without Tears or D'Nealian to help plan for this.

- *Adjusted tables and chairs* that are at the appropriate level for each student. Consult your custodian for assistance. You might also offer a footstool to a student whose chair is so tall that her legs are swinging in the air.

- *Pencil grips* that help support a young writer working to ingrain his pencil grip into his muscle memory, knowingly or not. You might think immediately of the hard plastic triangle grip or the squishy one that looks like a pencil cozy. Most occupational therapists agree that these are not helpful. Instead, look for pencil grips with clear indents where the fingers are meant to go. These pencil grips include the Start Right, the Grotto, and the Stetro.

- *Fat markers* or other writing tools that encourage proper finger placement.

- *A variety of writing surfaces.* Some students work best while writing on a vertical or elevated surface because it helps support the muscles in the wrist while others work best at a traditional tabletop parallel to the floor. (More about this later.)

There is a slightly larger challenge to help students in grades 3–5 who are struggling with posture and pencil grip, in part because by the time most students reach third grade, the pencil grip and posture have become so ingrained that they are incredibly challenging to unlearn. So, aside from storming your primary colleagues and demanding they teach the requisite five minutes of handwriting with the appropriate pencil grips, what can you do? Here are a few simple ways to support these writers:

- *Just as with the K–2 students, ensure that every student has access to an appropriately adjusted table or writing surface.* Besides enlisting the help of the custodian, you might also offer alternative spaces in the classroom during writing time where the tables are of different sizes than the majority.

- *Offer vertical writing spaces.* Some teachers use slant boards in order to elevate a student's wrist and offer it support, especially for students who are writing with a hooked arm. If slant boards are hard to find or too expensive, a simple, four- to five-inch three-ring binder used with the narrow end facing the student will suffice.

- *Provide pencil grips*, such as the Stetro. Although they may not correct long-ingrained finger placement, they can make writing more comfortable for some students.

For Students Who Apply a Lot of Pressure to the Pencil

At first glance, these students might not seem to have an obvious issue. They might have nice handwriting or produce a lot of writing. Yet over a stretch of time the hand will get fatigued far earlier than is necessary. For these students, some of the easiest modifications involve altering materials that are offered during writing time:

- Offer felt-tip pens. The ink shows up clearly with little pressure, keeping students from pressing down just to make sure their words are seen. Additionally, felt-tip pens can be difficult to use, or create ink spots when pressed on too hard, allowing a student to self-correct for pressure.

- If you cannot imagine a writing workshop without pencils, offer .5 lead mechanical pencils, which, while very grown-up feeling and exciting for the writer, will not support much pressure before breaking. This will help the student become better at self-monitoring the amount of pressure she is using.

- Have the student try placing his paper on a soft place-mat or carpet square and writing on that. If the student uses too much pressure, the pencil will push through the paper, encouraging the student to self-monitor the amount of pressure needed to make a legible mark.

When the Student Still Seems to Be Struggling

There are some students for whom none of the previous strategies will offer much relief. For those students, whose needs might go beyond poor pencil grip or weak wrist strength, we might decide to look for help in the technological realm. Often these students will write primarily on keyboards in their adult life because of the nature of the handwriting issues. Most of the occupational therapists I met with agreed that keyboarding is most appropriate to begin with older students whose fingers are long enough to comfortably reach across the keys. They also insist that the student is taught proper keyboarding position and technique. If you feel that you have a possible candidate for keyboarding, whether on a laptop, an AlphaSmart, or some other keyboarding technology, you will want to seek the advice of an occupational therapist.

Your Reflections

Perhaps you are right now thinking of all the students you've taught who have talked about their hurting hands. You might have tried some of the strategies mentioned here with some of them, and you may have been stumped about how to proceed with others.

Take some time to jot down the names of the students in your class whom you have heard say, "My hand hurts," or who have in other ways shown you that writing can be a grueling, sometimes physically uncomfortable experience.

Then jot down your plans for next steps in working with each of these students. Have you already observed the student writing, looked carefully at samples of his written work, and interviewed him? Which of the strategies mentioned in this chapter have you tried? Which ones have been successful? Are there new ones you want to try?

Recently I was working in a middle school classroom where a student was not writing. When I asked him what was happening, he said, "My hand hurts."

"Oh," I said. "My hand hurts too sometimes. Would you like me to teach you some things you can do to make it better?"

He looked at me rather strangely. "Uh, no. I just need to rest it. I'll be fine in a minute."

He made me smile, knowing that often the adage is correct—sometimes the best solutions are the simplest ones.

CHAPTER THREE

"I don't know how to spell."

His former teachers told me that Jonathan didn't write. "I don't know how he's going to survive in *your* class," one of them joked. So, for the whole first week of school, I watched him for a few minutes of each writing workshop on high alert. I noticed that he would dutifully pull out his writing notebook, sharpen his pencil to needle width, and then place the date on the top of the page. He would carefully write the first word, *The* or *One*. Then he would stop. He would stare off into space. He would ask to sharpen his pencil again. By the end of the writing workshop, Jonathan would not have more than a few words on his paper unless an adult intervened.

Then one day I noticed he was busily writing away in his notebook as he sat on the rug. I looked over his shoulder excitedly, thinking he must have been inspired by something. What I saw soon made a lot of sense. He was copying the class chart from the minilesson.

After talking at length with him, noticing his writing was composed almost entirely of sight words and words from our word wall or charts, and noticing the absence of any spelling errors in his writing, I realized that Jonathan was afraid to write anything down unless he could be absolutely certain it was spelled correctly. Perhaps you have a student like Jonathan in your class.

Or perhaps you recognize Hannah. She always sat with perfect posture, hands neatly folded. Her notebooks were filled with mechanical pencil writing that was so light and tentative, it was difficult to read. And, most telling, I could not walk anywhere near her table without her hand flying into the air and her asking, "How do you spell . . . ?"

It is tempting to say that these students were the products of a school that overemphasized mechanics and spelling at the cost of meaning and craft. Or perhaps they came from parents who really pressured them about spelling. But neither of those things was true. Both of these students—in fact, almost all the students in my class—had been in my school since kindergarten, where healthy writing workshops could be found in every classroom. Yet they struggled to put any words on paper that they did not know without a shadow of a doubt were spelled correctly.

Now that I have the opportunity to be in so many classrooms for my work with the Teachers College Reading and Writing Project, I see the patterns from my own classroom playing out again and again when it comes to spelling. When a student is not willing to write a word that she does not know how to spell, it is difficult for her to put *anything* down on paper, let alone something meaningful and perhaps risky.

Clearly this is a major hurdle for any student trying to write with fluency and confidence.

Recognizing Students Who Are Struggling with Spelling

Struggling spellers are perhaps some of the easiest for teachers to identify. Just as with all the other students discussed in this book, you will want to first observe the student, look at the student's work, and make sure to have a conversation with her in order to gain a full picture of what she is thinking and doing and attempting to do.

Besides the obvious question "How do you spell . . . ?" there are some other telltale signs that will let you know there might be some work to do in supporting a writer with spelling:

▶ The student's eyes are often glued to a classroom tool that contains words she can use in her writing, whether it is the model from the minilesson, a word wall list, or charts around the room that contain a lot of high-frequency words.

▶ The student seems to write in spurts and stalls. The stalling happens in the middle of a word, with the pencil hovering after only a letter or two has been jotted down. Sometimes the student ends up replacing those initial letters with another word entirely, almost as if he has decided to use a synonym in order to avoid any spelling embarrassment.

- The student refuses to use any writing utensil that is not erasable.

- The student frequently asks, no matter what subject the class is studying, "Does spelling count?"

- The student's success on spelling tests and activities seems unrelated to his spelling in a writing piece.

When we observe any of these behaviors, they might not be indicative of a student who is a poor speller. In fact, these students sometimes pass as strong spellers precisely because they rarely make spelling mistakes. However, the behaviors do give us some insights into the student's anxiety level with regard to spelling. Clearly the student's anxiety level is high—and not just at editing time.

In order to get a clearer indication of how a student's spelling strategies and output play out, we need to look at his written work. Now, a few words of caution about looking at student work for spelling: The chances are pretty good, unless the student is one of those passing spellers, that we have already noticed that he has some struggles in spelling. However, we want to look at his work with fresh eyes. We want to see what strategies the student is trying to use, what he knows about how words work, and if spelling seems to be getting in the way of other aspects of writing.

A few things we might keep in mind while looking at student work:

- Does the student erase or cross out a lot? Or does it appear that she does not make corrections, even if the word is misspelled?

▶ Does the student use only sight words or class words when writing?

▶ Does the student *ever* make a spelling error? If not, does the variety in vocabulary use closely represent the student's spoken language?

▶ When there are misspellings, are the words misspelled consistently throughout the piece? Or are they spelled differently each time?

▶ When looking at misspellings, can you determine what spelling strategy the student was using? Was he trying to sound it out? Was he recalling from memory letters he might have seen in his reading, even if the letters aren't all there or in the right order? Was he over-generalizing a rule, such as always adding *es* when making words plural?

By looking closely at what the student knows to do with her spelling work, we can begin to determine her strengths, speculate on her prior experience with spelling strategies, and consider her own awareness of her spelling struggles. We can also use this information to start our interview by beginning with a compliment. We might say, "I was looking over your writing last night and I was impressed with what you do when you are trying to spell a tricky word. It looks like you try to focus in on how the word sounds and try to include every letter you hear when you say the word out loud. Is that right?"

We might then ask questions about what the student knows about spelling as well as what she feels about it:

- ▶ What do you do when you are trying to spell a tricky word?

- ▶ What kinds of words do you find tricky?

- ▶ When you are writing and want to use a particular word you don't know how to spell, do you ever substitute another word that you do know how to spell? If so, how often does that happen?

- ▶ How important do you feel spelling is?

- ▶ Do you ever have a hard time remembering how to spell a word that you used to know?

- ▶ Do you ever choose a different topic or story to write about because the first topic or story has too many words that you don't know how to spell?

After our conversation with the student, we should have a good idea of what strategies the student knows to use, even if she doesn't always use them. We should also know a little bit more about how spelling does or does not get in the way of the writer generating and drafting text.

We can then take this information and begin to create our teaching plan. While every chapter in this book takes on writing issues that can be taught on a whole-class level, spelling in particular lends itself to a wider audience. As you read the following strategies, think of how some of them might be turned into lessons the whole class can learn from.

Strategies for Helping Students Who Struggle with Spelling

As I have heard linguist and educator Sandra Wilde joke, "There are only two places people expect perfection: brain surgery and spelling." It is for precisely that reason—the idea that in our society people are judged, fairly or not, by their spelling—that we need to teach students how to spell with relative accuracy, or at least the ability to make smart mistakes. On the other hand, we need to be vigilant in ensuring that we balance spelling instruction with an emphasis on the creative and generative work that kids oftentimes find blocked by concerns over spelling.

That said, the following suggestions are based on my work with the teachers at P.S. 18 and P.S. 94, suggestions from my colleagues at the Reading and Writing Project, and ideas from three major thinkers in the realm of spelling: Sandra Wilde, Diane Snowball, and Donald Bear.

Consider Your Spelling Curriculum

When considering the effect spelling has on writing, it is important to think about how (or, in some cases, *if*) spelling is addressed as its own subject in our classrooms.

▶ Does your school have a consistent spelling curriculum (not necessarily a program, although it could be)?

▶ Do you teach spelling regularly, several times a week, in short, focused sessions where students are actively engaged?

▶ Do you encourage students to take a few seconds to figure out words they already know how to spell rather than write them any-which-way or do you suggest they save correct spelling until the edit?

Sandra Wilde (2008) argues that since there is little proof that memorizing lists of words has ever helped make a strong speller, we should instead focus our energy on teaching students how words work and strategies for figuring out how to spell tricky words. For example, we might show students how to think of words that work in similar ways in order to figure out how to spell them.

Research also shows that we do not need to spend more than several minutes each day on spelling. As long as it is concentrated, active, purposeful, and transferable, students will benefit from it. One option might be to spend a few minutes every Monday introducing a concept. Then each day during the week, spend a few minutes engaged in activities that explore and practice that spelling strategy or concept, ending with a wrap-up on Friday.

It is also important to think about spelling curriculum in writing workshop time, not just spelling time. Lucy Calkins says that it is crucial for us to teach students to pause when they get to a tricky word while brainstorming, drafting, or even revising and think, "Do I know how to spell this?" If the student does know how to spell the word or has a strategy for figuring it out quickly (such as looking at the word wall), she should make a good effort to spell the word accurately in the midst of composing. Otherwise we are piling up the work to do during editing time, making it much more likely we will be overwhelmed by the sheer amount of it—much of it work we could have tackled in a few seconds during the drafting process.

Teach How Words Work and How Writers Work to Spell Words

It will never do to have students come to us whenever they have a spelling challenge. In the first place, it is not practical to have twenty-plus kids rushing toward us during workshop time. More importantly, our students will not always have us with them. We need to be sure they have spelling strategies they can access regardless of the classroom or even the writing situation.

One of the most time-saving strategies to teach is to identify which words it makes sense to stop and figure out how to spell before continuing to write. These words include sight words, words the class has studied, and words that have familiar patterns. These are words students know how to spell but have not yet begun to spell with automaticity. We should teach students that spelling those words correctly the first time can save them a lot of time later on.

We can teach students how to use the margins of their paper to try different ways to figure out a spelling, such as Diane Snowball and Faye Bolton's (1999) have-a-go strategy, where students try to write a word out three different ways until they find one that looks right. Strategies like this allow a writer to quickly eyeball a word and then move on with writing.

Perhaps one of the most important spelling-while-composing lessons to teach is what to do when one encounters a very tricky word whose spelling is going to take a little research to uncover. I show students how I often place a small question mark or other marker (some teachers prefer the initials *SP*) above the word I want to use while drafting when I know that it's going to take more than a few seconds to figure out how to spell it. Then, when checking on the word won't get in the way of my generating process, I'll do a little research on the word's spelling.

Introduce Tools That Can Become Lifelong Resources

Perhaps one of the most important things to keep in mind when teaching students about spelling while writing is how we, as adult writers, spell words we don't know. Often we forget that some of the strategies we teach students are impractical or strategies that we seldom, if ever, use. For example, very few teachers I know who have a spelling concern while putting up a bulletin board will head into the classroom to grab the dictionary!

Instead, we might study the tools we use to help make us more accurate spellers and consider how to bring them into our classrooms. We can begin by creating a space in our classrooms for students to use the various tools that we actually use as writers and spellers.

For example, every time I've worked with a copyeditor, he or she has written all over my drafts with different-colored pens or pencils and asked me to use the same bright colors when I responded to his or her edits. Most often, we use blue, but I've seen and used purple, green, and even red. The ink allows corrections to pop, making it more likely that the writer will be able to see his own corrections. Another cool side effect of the pens? Kids love gimmicks and new things. With a gel pen in hand, many students find more mistakes than we ever could have imagined possible.

Another tool is one that most of us cannot imagine living without yet was not even in common use until fairly recently: spell-checkers. When I ask most adults who call themselves bad spellers how they still manage to write so much, they say, "I use a spell-checker." And yet many of our students never have access to these vital tools. Depending on the resources of your school, you might be able to have students use the spell-checkers that are built into computer word-processing programs. However, there are also small, handheld ones that can be placed on a writing shelf or even in a basket on each table. One caveat: it's important that we introduce these tools to our students with care and make part of our work showing when it makes sense to use them and how to determine which word is the correct spelling for the writer's purpose.

A third tool that we sometimes take for granted is a print-rich environment. The more you read, the more exposure you have to the ways words work. Many adults, when struggling to spell a word, quickly scan their environment on the off-hand chance that the desired word is there. When our classrooms offer plenty of charts, signs, books, word walls, and other texts, we can be sure that our students are being exposed to the written word and all of its quirks on a daily basis.

Finally, perhaps the most handy tool we have and yet probably the one we teach students to use the least is spelling experts. Admit it. Not too long ago, you were working on a chart in your classroom or writing a quick note to a parent while standing in the school office or maybe slaving away at that bulletin board in the hallway. You were in either one camp or another: you yelled down the hallway to ask a colleague how to spell a word, or a colleague was yelling down the hallway to ask you. Adults ask people how to spell words all the time. We should teach our students when and how to ask someone else for help when spelling a word. This is certainly one of those strategies our students will use for a lifetime.

Your Reflections

After reading this chapter, you might be thinking of your own Jonathans and Hannahs. Or perhaps you've grappled with your own struggles around spelling.

Take a couple of minutes to jot down the names of the students in your class whom you have heard say, "I'm not a good speller," or who you know feel that way. Are there a lot of names? Or just a few?

Then jot down your plans for next steps in working with spelling. Do you need to make large curriculum changes? Or small classroom environment changes? Do you need to re-examine the language that you use? Or do you simply need to be more systematic in your approach to spelling? Think about what will be the first things you can implement.

Jonathan's worries about spelling continued for a good part of the year, until I could convince him that he already knew quite a lot about spelling. "You know so much about how words begin and how words end, and there are hundreds more words you know how to spell correctly."

Jonathan looked skeptical, but he kept listening to me as I went on to show him how he could put down everything he knew about spelling a word while he was writing and then mark the word so that he could go back and try to figure it out later. He did decide to try the strategy, and for the most part it helped him, at least while generating ideas, combat his fear of putting any words down on the paper. I'd like to tell you that by the end of his year with me he became a strong and confident speller, and he did improve. However, Jonathan did not leave my classroom having mastered the spelling hurdle. But he did leave knowing how to keep spelling from interfering with his strong and confident *writing*.

CHAPTER FOUR

"I don't have anything to write about."

I don't believe in writer's block.

I believe that writers who do not know what to write, who can't begin to even put the first word to paper, who stare at the ceiling and then back to the paper, hoping something will magically appear are not blocked in an irretrievable, let's-just-hang-up-our-pens way.

I believe they just haven't yet been given the tools to fill the fearsome blank page with words.

As writing workshop teachers, we struggle to create classrooms where students live like writers in the way Lucy Calkins discusses in her book *Living Between the Lines* (1990). Writers who carry notebooks with them everywhere in order to collect every little scrap of something that maybe can be turned into a piece of writing later. Writers who collect stories the way some people collect Hummel. Writers who are constantly working on their next writing project and planning ahead for the one after that.

And yet, many of us, in our rush to get through curriculum, meet standards, and prepare students for tests, often skip past those teaching points about living the life of a writer. We just don't have time for them. Besides, most of our students don't seem to really need them. When we walk around our classrooms, we see heads tucked, pens moving. Our students don't need to live like writers. We have a deadline to meet!

Then we see one, two, sometimes more pens frozen. Or we hear the pencil sharpener start to whirr for the eleventh time in ten minutes. Or we pull up a chair next to a student to confer and when we ask her what she's working on, she looks us straight in the eye and says, "I don't have anything to write about."

Understanding Why Students Are Getting Stuck

As I've argued throughout this book, in order to even discuss ways of getting students unstuck, we need to first know how writing goes for these students. We need to observe them when they're writing and when they are not. We need to read their writing. We need to talk to them.

If you know a student who is often sitting in front of a blank page, start your work of helping the student by spending a few minutes watching him during writing time. Following are some things you might look for:

▶ Does the student refer to charts in the classroom while writing?

- Does the student go back into his notebook or folder and reread old pieces of writing?

- Does the student cover up his blank page with his arm?

- Does the student look over the shoulders of his classmates to see what they are working on?

- Does the student wander around the classroom during writing time, picking up books or hanging out in the writing center?

- Does the student get stuck only when writing?

- Does the student usually get stuck at certain times, such as after lunch or on Monday mornings?

Noticing these things will help you get an idea of what tools the student is already using or not using. Doing so will also give you a general idea as to what the student's attitude is toward writing and whether or not he has already developed some strategies of his own that you can capitalize on. For example, I might teach the wandering student that writers sometimes take walks to clear their minds or stare out of windows to get inspired. I might encourage the student to try using those strategies when he gets stuck.

Next, spend some time with the student's writing. Gather up any notebooks, folders, and finished pieces you can find. If possible, see if you can find any writing from previous years. Then, holding some of the theories you have begun to form based on your observations, you might look for some of the following:

- ▶ Does the student have any topics that he returns to a lot, such as friends, horses, Grandpa?

- ▶ Does the student seem to have more writing in any particular genre?

- ▶ Does the student's notebook or folder have a lot of blank pages where there should be writing?

- ▶ Does the student have torn-out pages?

- ▶ Does the student's writing sound generic and lack meaning?

- ▶ Does the student have hidden writing pieces that are about topics such as farts or written in a genre such as comic strips, that is unlikely to be expected in your classroom?

Based on what you see in the writing, you might consider a whole additional piece to the puzzle. You might notice that the student hasn't quite found a topic he's interested in or perhaps he's not ready to take writing risks and write about topics that are near and dear to him. You might notice that the student doesn't seem to realize that some of the topics he writes about repeatedly can be go-to topics when he's stuck.

Finally, take your growing theories about the student and have a conversation with him. Here are some things you might want to include in the conversation:

- ▶ I notice you write a lot about *x* [topic]. Tell me about that.

- ▶ What's important to you in your life?

▶ When you get stuck finding something to write about, what do you do?

▶ When you look at all your writing pieces, which one is your favorite? Why?

▶ Where do you think other people get their ideas for writing?

▶ How often do you write outside of school?

▶ Do you carry a writer's notebook any place besides home and school?

Depending on how the student answers, you might discover that, in fact, he knows a lot of strategies for generating ideas, but he simply hasn't figured out how to apply them to his own writing life. On the other hand, you may discover that he sees writing as a complete mystery and has yet to find his idea-gathering sweet spot that he can return to again and again.

Strategies for Helping Students Develop a Repertoire of Ways to Generate Ideas

After gathering all the information we can, we should have a general sense of many things about this struggling writer, as well as some very specific ideas that will help narrow down the kinds of strategies we might want to teach. The plan of action will be based on at least a few of the following:

- the student's passions
- the student's past successes
- the student's knowledge and use of strategies that were taught in the past
- the student's areas of frustration

The plan of action should be seen as a means for this student to be able to *independently* access a variety of strategies for a variety of different writing pieces. It is important to avoid giving the student the impression that she cannot come up with ideas on her own.

Cultivate a Classroom Where Passions Are Honored

Some teachers create a culture that honors students' passions by allowing each student to have a small square of bulletin board space where she can post favorite quotes, photographs, pieces of work, lists of favorite books, or even artifacts from a passion, such as ticket stubs from a basketball game. Other teachers draw on Georgia Heard's (1998) idea of creating maps of the heart, maps of the things that are really important to students, early in the school year so that they can refer to those maps all year long for inspiration. Still other teachers simply allow for some talk time on Friday afternoon when students can share their interests and stories with each other, becoming known to their community as skateboarders or gamers or dog lovers.

It does not matter particularly how we bring students' passions into our classroom. What does matter is that we carve out space to notice and admire students for their passions. This not only allows us to see them as fully fleshed human beings but also allows students to see that these outside passions can have a home at school, especially in writing workshop.

Offer Students Regular Opportunities for Writing Reflection

Many of us used to include, as part of the publishing process, an opportunity for students to reflect in writing on their finished writing pieces, as part of our assessment work. I've noticed that lately, as more and more of us are integrating rubrics into our practice, fewer and fewer of us are having students spend time reflecting on their writing. The two do not have to be mutually exclusive.

You might want to create a quick, short-answer form that gives students a few guided questions to get them started, such as "How did you get your idea for writing this piece?" or "What was the best part of the writing process for you?" You can also simply pass out blank pieces of loose-leaf paper that students can use to write free-form reflections. Or you might include as part of every writing celebration a chance for students to talk in partnerships or clubs about their experiences.

By offering these opportunities to reflect, we not only gain valuable insight into each student's feelings about a piece but also create a habit of mind. Writers reflect regularly. And it is often in the reflecting on a recently finished piece that the seeds of new pieces are born or else mistakes are more easily avoided in the future. For instance, a child might realize that he really enjoyed writing his poetry anthology about baseball and then consider using baseball as the jumping-off point for his upcoming memoir.

Offer Several Idea-Generating Strategies

As more and more teachers work together across grades to align curriculum often there are set strategies that we want all students to know and use. The challenge, then, is to try to separate out for ourselves what is the skill that we're focusing on and what is the strategy. Often we can get so tied up in the strategy that we lose sight of the skill.

For example, one strategy I have seen teachers teach comes from the work of Ralph Fletcher. In the simplest form, we show students how they can quickly sketch a place of importance to them and then use that sketch to help find story ideas. I have often seen teachers teach that lesson, then circulate the room, ensuring that each student is using the strategy and is using it effectively. If a student is either struggling with the strategy or not using it at all, the teacher will confer with that student until he has mastered the strategy. This, in some ways, is a very instinctive teaching model. After all, isn't it important to teach for mastery? However, we can break it down a little by asking ourselves, "What is the writing skill that I want the students to practice? Do they (or I) know any other strategies that can also be used to get to that skill?"

With the aforementioned sketch strategy, the skill I hope the student uses is to generate ideas for personal narratives. I can assume that my students already have a repertoire of strategies for generating ideas for personal narratives from my teaching alone. That's not even taking into account any strategies they might know from other teachers or simply being inspired to write about a certain time.

One way to address this issue is by looking at the closing, or link, of the minilesson. When I was teaching a minilesson, after I had explained the strategy I was modeling and was ready to send the students back to their seats, I would say something along the lines of, "So, writers, you now have one more strategy you can try when you are trying to generate personal narrative ideas. You also know other strategies such as listing people who matter to you and being inspired by literature. Put a thumb up if you are going to try the sketch strategy today. Put a thumb up if you are going to use another strategy."

In addition to tucking in and expecting students to choose different strategies, you might also want to take a quick tour of your classroom to see if you have charts or other tools that remind students of strategies they already know (see Figure 4.1).

Collect a Variety of Generating Strategies to Teach

Of course, it's much easier to teach a man to fish if you know more than one way to fish. After all, what if he doesn't have a pole? What if he lives near the ocean and you've only ever taught people how to fish in lakes?

When I was first learning how to teach writing, I knew only a few generating strategies for each unit I taught. They were the strategies I'd learned from professional development workshops or books that I'd read. I taught them in my minilessons. If a student had trouble with one of them, I used my conference time to reteach the minilesson strategy, even if it clearly didn't work for the student, because that strategy was the only one I had, not necessarily the best one for the student. The procedure of narrow teaching and repetitive

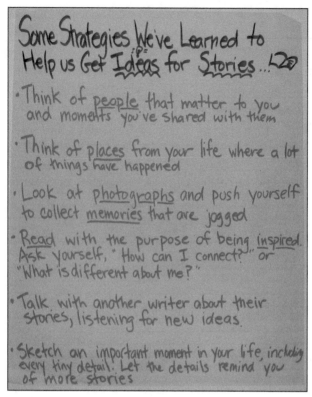

FIG. 4.1 *Strategy Chart*

reteaching led to frustration for both the students and me. With time I realized that one of the best ways to differentiate instruction for my students was to pick the most accessible teaching points for my minilessons and then gather a bank of other strategies I could teach in conferences and small groups.

Thinking about how to collect a wide array of strategies for the various units you plan to teach across the year can be a bit intimidating at first. Following are a few tips for collecting generating strategies as well as some go-to strategies that can be used again and again by students and teachers alike:

▶ My favorite way to gather generating strategies is probably the one we forget first, and yet it is perhaps the most limitless source we can find: We can write. And we can watch ourselves as we write. When we are inspired to begin a story, or a poem, we can ask ourselves what we were doing—what sparked us? We can then use those moments when we teach our children. I would be hard-pressed to think of any more authentic teaching than that.

▶ Another way to gather strategies is to read professional books for teachers with an eye for teaching points. Here is a partial list of a few of my favorite texts to return to again and again when on the hunt for writing-strategy inspiration:
  • *The Resourceful Writing Teacher*, by Jenny Bender (2007)
  • *The No-Nonsense Guide to Teaching Writing*, by Judy Davis and Sharon Hill (2003)
  • *Craft Lessons*, by Ralph Fletcher and JoAnn Portalupi (2007)
  • *The Writing Workshop*, by Katie Wood Ray (2001)

▶ We might also read some professional books for writers. Granted, these books are written with adult writers in mind, so we need to make adaptations in terms of language, difficulty, and appropriateness. However, books written for professional writers offer a plethora of fresh ideas for any writer who is struggling to find something to write about. These are just a handful of books I refer to often, including

- *What If?* by Anne Bernays and Pamela Painter (2003)
- *Imaginative Writing,* by Janet Burroway (2006)
- *Steering the Craft,* by Ursula Le Guin (1998)
- *The Plot Thickens,* by Noah Lukeman (2003)
- *On Writing Well,* by William Zinsser (2006)

▶ Consider that almost every strategy you know can be adapted to meet the needs of another genre. For example, a common personal narrative strategy is to think of important people in your life and the stories connected to them. Students could also use that strategy to come up with ideas for a personal essay by thinking of important people in their lives and writing down their thoughts and feelings about them. Or for poetry, you might adapt the strategy to be about how poets can think of people who matter to them and then consider how to show their feelings with imagery and metaphor. See the chart on pages 56 and 57 for more examples.

Avoid Overcoaching of Writing

One of the most common sentences I've heard uttered across the country in almost every school I've worked in is "If I'm not sitting right next to him, he gets nothing done."

I have no doubt the statement is true. I certainly said and believed it of many of my own students. However, I am beginning to think that we are part of the problem of dependence. If a student rarely, if ever, gets a chance to daydream and wander and stumble onto a great idea, or else actively skim different strategy charts and harangue friends for ideas, when is the child ever going to learn how to cultivate that generative side of writing?

I've pulled up alongside many a student who was sitting in front of a blank page, claiming writer's block, and made the mistake of saying, "OK, Sasha. I see you're stuck. Have you tried writing about your new baby brother yet? Or how about your soccer game yesterday? I heard it was a great game." One of two things would happen in one of those conferences. The student might be resistant to all of my ideas, saying they were boring or stupid. Or—and in some ways this is worse because at least in the first scenario the student still had spirit—the student would take one of my suggestions, only to need another idea during our next cycle. She would never develop independence this way.

Another valuable lesson Lucy Calkins teaches, which I feel I should have tattooed on my forearm, is *teach the writer, not the writing*. In other words, whenever we are teaching a student, we should always be thinking, "What can I teach this student that he can use again in the future if he should ever find himself in this situation again?" The concept, while deceivingly difficult to execute regularly, is the literary equivalent of "Give a man a fish, and he eats for a day. Teach a man to fish, and he eats for a lifetime."

Personal Narrative	Informational *how-to, all-about, etc.*	Persuasive *essay, op-ed, speech, letter*	Fiction *realistic, historical, fantasy, etc.*	Poetry
Think of places that matter to you and the stories of your life that took place there. For example: "The time I went to the playground with my brother and he taught me how to turn flips on the jungle gym."	Think about the places that matter to you and what you can teach people about them. For example: "How to Use Playground Equipment Safely" or "All About Playgrounds"	Think about the places that matter to you and advocate for them. For example: "We need to save our playground!" or a letter to the mayor asking for more swings.	Think about the places that matter to you and stories that you can imagine happening there or places like it. For example, "A girl is lonely so she goes to the playground, where she makes a friend" or "A boy climbs on a slide on the playground, but instead of sliding down the chute, he finds himself in a whole new world."	Think about the places that matter to you and observe them with a poet's eyes. For example: "The playground is filled with bars. Cold bars. They remind me of my guinea pig's cage."
Look around the space where you are writing. Let the surroundings remind you of stories you could write. For example : "I see a flag hanging over the chalkboard. That reminds me of the Fourth of July party when I got stung by a bee."	Look around the space where you are writing. Let the surroundings remind you of things you could teach. For example: "I see a flag. I could teach people how to take care of a flag, or I could teach people about the different kinds of flags."	Look around the space where you are writing. Let the surroundings remind you of things you feel strongly about and want other people to care about too. For example: "I see a flag. I want to write a speech explaining to children why we should honor veterans with flags."	Look around the space where you are writing. Let the surroundings give you ideas for characters or plots you can turn into a story. For example: "I see a flag. I could write a story about a boy who wants to be in the color guard but can't because the Scout leader thinks he's too clumsy to hold the flag."	Look around the space where you are writing. Let the surroundings give you ideas for poems you might want to write. For example: "I see a flag. I could write about how I feel whenever I see the flag."

Collect a box or folder of photographs from your own life and those clipped from magazines. Look through the folder and see what stories the pictures remind you of.	Collect a box or folder of photographs from your own life and those clipped from magazines. Look through the folder and see what you'd like to teach other people about.	Collect a box or folder of photographs from your own life and those clipped from magazines. Look through the folder and see what ideas you can get that you feel strongly about and would like to convince other people to feel strongly about too.	Collect a box or folder of photographs from your own life and those clipped from magazines. Look through the folder and see what story ideas come to your mind.	Collect a box or folder of photographs from your own life and those clipped from magazines. Look through the folder and see what topics you'd like to explore in poetry.
Read examples of personal narrative from professional writers. Try to decide how you think they got their ideas for their stories, then try those strategies yourself.	Read examples of informational books from professional writers. Try to decide how you think they got their ideas for their writing, then try those strategies yourself.	Read examples of op-eds (speeches, letters) from professional writers. Try to decide how you think they got their ideas for their writing, then try those strategies yourself.	Read examples of fiction from professional writers. Try to decide how you think they got their story ideas for their writing, then try those strategies yourself.	Read examples of poetry from professional writers. Try to decide how you think they got their ideas for their writing, then try those strategies yourself.
Reread your writer's notebook or the stories in your folder. See if you can find any patterns that you can add to. For example: "I have a lot of stories about my ferrets in my notebook. So maybe my next entry can be a new ferret story."	Reread your writer's notebook or the stories in your folder. See if you can find any patterns that can give you ideas for topics to write about. For example: "I have a lot of stories about my ferrets in my notebook. So maybe my informational book could be about pet ferrets."	Reread your writer's notebook or the stories in your folder. See if you can find any patterns that can give you ideas on what to write about. For example: "I have a lot of stories about my ferrets in my notebook. So maybe my speech could be about pet ferrets and how they are terribly misunderstood."	Reread your writer's notebook or the stories in your folder. See if you can find any patterns that can give you ideas for stories to write about. For example: "I have a lot of stories about my ferrets in my notebook. So maybe my fantasy story could be about a talking ferret who is like a guide for my hero."	Reread your writer's notebook or the stories in your folder. See if you can find any patterns that can give you ideas for topics to write poetry about. For example: "I have a lot of stories about my ferrets in my notebook. So maybe I can start turning some of those entries into poems about ferrets."

Your Reflections

One of the most challenging things for a writer to contend with is a lack of ideas. It is also one of the hardest things for a writing teacher to contend with.

Take a couple of minutes to jot down the names of the students in your class whom you have heard say, "I don't have anything to write about."

Then jot down your plans for next steps in working with each of these students. Have you already interviewed and observed the student or do you still need to do that? What are you already doing to support this student in developing a repertoire of strategies to generate ideas? What else would you like to try?

Once you have adopted the attitude that there is no such thing as writer's block—just a writer who hasn't found the right strategy for him—you will find your attitude is contagious.

CHAPTER FIVE

"I never get to write anything I want to write."

I looked out over the twenty-eight eager sets of fourth-grade eyes. The students had just published last Friday, so they knew today was the day they would find out the new unit of study. "Today we are beginning some really exciting work. It's a new genre that none of you have ever done before." I paused for emphasis.

I could see a few students exchanging glances, others wiggling on the floor. "It's a genre that people write in all the way through school, through college, and even after that. It is called . . . essay!"

Most of the students grinned even further. I heard a loud "Yes!" and another student saying, "We're going to be doing college writing." I drank in their excitement, getting more enthused by the minute. Until I saw Theo in the background. His eyes were downcast. He was picking at the rug.

Sure enough, after the students were back at their seats, collecting ideas for possible essays, Theo didn't even have his notebook open. I plopped down next to him and said, "I noticed you're not writing, Theo. What's going on?"

He glanced up at me, then back down at his closed notebook, covered in skateboard stickers and photographs of his dog. He shook his head.

"Do you know why you're not writing?" I asked, a little bit quieter now, worried that maybe something was going on at home or he was having a fight with a friend. He looked so heartbroken.

He took a deep breath and then said, "I never get to write anything I want to write."

Understanding Why Students Are Not Feeling Drawn to the Genres We Are Teaching

Not every student who feels like Theo did is able to articulate it as well. As I suggested in earlier chapters, we need to begin our investigation with research. We need to observe students while they write, read their work, and have conversations with them.

Sometimes students who are uninspired by our curriculum choices simply sit motionless during writing workshop. Other times they display many of the behaviors discussed in other chapters—spending all their time on carefully written dates, repeatedly requesting to go to the bathroom, staring at blank pages. Or sometimes we mistake their comments for disrespectfulness. While we're enthusiastically teaching a lesson on increasing tension in our personal narratives, they're mumbling under their breath, "How come we never get to write fiction?"

Their notebooks are often stuffed with writing we never taught. There are stories of dragons and gunfights and song lyrics. There are letters to friends and attempts at comic strips tucked in between our carefully planned units of study.

If any of these scenarios sounds familiar, then you might want to follow up with a few conversational questions to get a better idea of how to reach the student. I try to avoid yes-or-no questions whenever possible, since I want to open up the dialogue.

- What was your favorite unit we studied this year? Why?

- What was your least favorite unit? Why?

- When you write in your free time, what sorts of things do you write?

- When you look through your notebook, which ones are your favorite entries? Tell me about them.

- What do you enjoy reading?

- What do you not like to read?

- If you had all the time and paper you needed, what would you write?

The answers to these questions, and others like them, will offer insights into what choices a student would make if she had the opportunity. It will also allow you to do some reflecting on where and how your teaching has been meeting her needs and where you might want to revise or refine some instructional plans. You can then reflect on what you need to address on either an individual basis or a whole-class one.

Strategies for Helping Students Develop a Sense of Agency and Independence

I remember, along with many longtime workshop teachers, years ago, when there were no curriculum calendars for writing. I remember spending months on memoirs and then several more months on poetry, only to find myself deciding midyear to try the feature article study my colleague down the hall had just tried. As long as my students kept writer's notebooks (often collecting for a solid month before choosing a seed idea to flesh out) and were using the writing process, I considered my workshop a success.

Then I learned about the idea of curriculum calendars. We could teach students specific skills for writing and teach them in units, much like the way we taught a multiplication unit in math or the water cycle in science. It felt revolutionary. It felt solid. It was both.

Time has passed now, and I'm seeing more and more schools develop grade-by-grade curriculum calendars. They allow for consistency, reinforcement, mastery, and a gradual introduction of progressively more sophisticated skill sets. The curriculum calendars that these schools are developing allow us to make sure we're meeting state standards, preparing students for tests, and, most importantly, giving students rich opportunities to explore and excel in writing.

Yet, as with all things educational, many of us have become so focused on our finely crafted units that we've forgotten about the lingering and exploration that allowed us to discover them in the first place. We move from teaching point to teaching point, unit to unit, hardly looking up from our calendars to see what our students are doing.

Clearly we should be teaching curriculum within units of study. However, there are also ways to bring some of the best, most inspirational work of the past into our curriculum.

In his book *Boy Writers*, Ralph Fletcher (2006) notes that many of our boys struggle through writing precisely because they don't see room for their interests, their stories, their ideas in the writing they do in school. And boys are not the only ones. Many students, both boys and girls, either take matters into their own hands and work on their own writing projects outside of school or they give up on writing entirely because it just doesn't seem to be for them.

When students ask us for the chance to write *anything*, we need to respond. We need to make it our business to show them that there is a place for everyone and his or her interests in writing.

But how do we balance curriculum pressures with choice?

In *Independent Writing* (2004), I argue that we don't need to toss aside curriculum calendars and writing skills in order to get students interested in writing. In fact, I suggest that units of study are precisely what students need in order to gain and maintain the skills they need to become successful in all their writing endeavors. We can also teach our students how to maintain active independent writing lives, much like they maintain active independent reading lives outside of reading workshop. We would be disappointed, if not shocked, to hear that each of our students wasn't reading something independently outside of our whole-class curriculum.

There are some simple things that we can incorporate right away in our writing workshops that will offer students plenty of choice and keep them at the heart of our workshops while utilizing our curriculum as our guide.

Create an Atmosphere of Independence

When a student complains that she never gets to write what she wants to write, it is perhaps one of the most mixed-blessing things she could say. On the one hand, our pride is a little bruised. We worked hard on our curriculum calendars in order to make them comprehensive and interesting. On the other hand, there is a small burst of joy in knowing that the student *wants to write*.

We owe it to that student, and any students like her who might not be as vocal, to offer plenty of opportunities for choice in our workshops. There are many ways we can incorporate independence—big and small—into our writing workshops. A simple way to begin is by allowing students to choose from a variety of writing strategies, not just the one taught in that day's minilesson. We can also encourage students to write in their notebooks every free moment they have, whenever the mood strikes, even if what they want to write about has nothing to do with the current study in the classroom.

We might also consider practices that we have always held tight reins on and refine them so that they can be utilized more independently by the students. For example, we might provide opportunities for students to choose their own mentor authors to learn from, outside of the ones we have introduced to the entire class.

We can also create models of independence in our classrooms. I like to make a big deal out of students who try new things in writing workshop, whether it's inventing a new strategy, experimenting with a new genre, or simply publishing in a unique way. Some teachers like to add those students' names to charts or highlight them in the class newsletter.

Develop Structures for Writers Who Need Support

For every student who immediately takes to the new levels of independence in the classroom, there is another student who does not feel confident enough to navigate them on his own. This does not mean the student is any less desirous of choice; it simply means that we need to offer additional scaffolds.

One of the easiest and most visible ways to do this is to develop a writing center that contains any supplies a writer might need to keep working on a project. Some things you might want to include in your writing center are a variety of papers, pens, pencils, sticky notes, highlighters, spell-checkers, scissors, tape, staplers, grammar guides, and books about writing.

Other teachers I know create typed-up versions of important charts that are no longer hanging in the classroom for students to place in their writing folders. For example,

"What to Do When You're Stuck" and "What Goes in Your Writer's Notebook?" would be great options for students who still need those charts from September but would never dare ask for them. You can also place those typed-up charts in the writing center for students to grab as needed.

An additional way to offer students support while nurturing their agency is by providing a sign-up list for students who would like to request a conference with you. By using this simple tool, students will know that if they have something really important to discuss with the teacher, they have some control over when that conversation will take place.

Cultivate Writing Partners and Clubs

The single most important support system we can help our students obtain and maintain is a relationship with peers. Writing, by its very nature, is a solitary affair. Our students need to know that writers regularly alleviate that loneliness, and elevate the quality of their writing, by sharing their work with peers. By cultivating these relationships in our own classrooms, we are enabling our students to see that long after they leave us, they will still have all the support they need in order to write. And, most importantly, when a writer has a support system, he is more likely to venture out on his own and try things that maybe he would not have tried before because they were not taught in class.

We can create these partnerships in a number of ways. Some teachers allow students to choose their own partners and groups. Other teachers match up students based on personality. Some pair up students based on complementary skills. Still others have each student write a letter about what he is looking for in a writing partner or club and then match up students based on those similarities. No matter which way you ultimately form your students into peer groups, it is important that every student has someone she can talk with.

Offer Opportunities to Publish Independently

Perhaps the most satisfying part of the writing process to any writer, child or adult, is holding the finished product in your hands. Yet, for many students, when they are working on a piece of writing outside of the class curriculum, it never moves beyond the pages of the notebook.

If we are to offer students choice, to tell them that they can and should write anything they want to write, then we also need to make sure that they have the opportunities needed to get those pieces of writing out in the world properly.

One of the simplest ways to do this is to set up a self-publishing center in the classroom. Give students access to construction paper, fancy publishing paper, staplers, markers, and anything else you typically provide to students when they publish. You might then create a self-publishing basket, where students can leave their latest masterpieces for you to read and make a big deal about. Some teachers even create a "Self-Published" bulletin board in the classroom on which to hang these pieces. I had such a bulletin board, as well as a monthly morning meeting where we would give a round of applause to all of the students who had self-published and then watch them ceremoniously pin their own pieces to the bulletin board using special thumbtacks reserved for just those pieces.

Your Reflections

When I first thought of struggling writers, I never thought of students who wanted to write but just didn't want to write what I was teaching. Now I'm realizing that they are often struggling not so much against the subject as they are against the constraints of curriculum.

Take a couple of minutes to jot down the names of the students in your own class whom you have heard say, "I never get to write anything I want to write."

Then jot down your plans for next steps in working with each of these students. Have you already interviewed and observed the student or do you still need to do that? What are you already doing to support this student in developing her own writing plans? Have you considered offering more opportunities for choice in your curriculum plans? How might you do that?

By the time I left the classroom, my students were regularly balancing the demands of my whole-class curricula, complete with genre studies and skills-based lessons, alongside their own independent writing goals and plans. I never again heard a student complain about not getting to write what he wanted to write.

CHAPTER SIX

"I'm done."

I had just put down my notes from the minilesson and was grabbing my conference clipboard. It was *at most* five minutes since I had sent the students back to their tables.

"I'm done," Evanna declared with finality.

I whizzed around, ready to say something pithy in response. Maybe something along the lines of "When you're done, you've just begun." But before I could get anything out of my mouth, another voice across the room chimed in, "I'm done, too."

And then to my horror, yet another voice sang out, "Me, too. Now what do I do?" It seemed to me that no other phrase had ever been uttered as loudly in my class as those two big words.

It wasn't even a revision lesson!

It can happen to us any day of the week, during any step in the writing process. We think we have set the students up with more writing work to do than they have time for, and yet . . .

Understanding the Desire to Be Done

First of all, it's important for us to be honest with ourselves. There *is* something intrinsically satisfying about having completed something. We punch out of the time clock, empty the last grocery bag, flip the final page of a novel, and feel very satisfied. One day I was chatting with Lester Laminack, author of several children's books and books for teachers. He was discussing how many writers he knew who liked to clean. "Why?" I asked. "*I* hate it."

"Because for us writers, we rarely ever get to finish anything. To see something like a sparkling kitchen, completely clean, is a very satisfying feeling. To be done with something at last!"

I realized that it was very true. That before I jumped down kids' throats, I should probably remember that for many of them, they were simply excited to be at a place where they could feel accomplished. It was certainly a feeling I could relate to all too well.

That said, there are also the students who, for reasons discussed elsewhere in this book, have not found that writing works for them. Getting done is very much akin to cleaning one's plate of liver and Brussels sprouts. They see each day's writing as something to get through and finish, much like a math worksheet or other assignment with a beginning and ending point. They haven't quite grasped the idea of writing as a process.

A third group of students who belong to the "I'm done" club are those students who do not have a long-term writing plan. They do not necessarily view themselves as writers, but they also do not hate to write. They simply do not have a vision of next steps when they have completed whatever they have set out to do. They lack what Carl Anderson calls *purpose*.

Of course, to determine which of these groups, or perhaps another group entirely, the student you are studying falls into, you'll want to first observe her. You'll want to ask the following questions:

- How is the student's work pace? Is it steady? Or rushed? Or stop and start?

- Does the student exhibit any of the avoidance behaviors explored in earlier chapters such as excessive pencil sharpening, asking for the bathroom pass, or hiding in her hoodie?

- What is the student's affect when she is working? Determined? Uninterested? Frustrated?

- What is the student's affect when she is declaring her finished status? Triumphant? Relieved? Concerned?

Once you've done some observation, you'll probably already have a ballpark idea of which camp this student mostly falls into, although, as with all things, the student's work probably falls into more than one category. To help get an even clearer picture, you might want to turn to her writing. Probably the best source of information for you would be either her folders or notebooks or any place else where there is work in progress, rather than finished pieces. You'll be looking for pace, stamina, process, and planning. Look through the student work for things such as the following:

- *Typical length of stories or entries.* Would you say the pieces fall into the average length for students in your class? Longer? Shorter?

- *Variety of topics written about.* Do you see that the student seems committed to certain topics? Or does she seem to prefer to write about a lot of different things?

- *Use of appropriate writing strategies.* Does the student's writing reflect what you are teaching daily? Does the writing show independent attempts at trying other strategies? Does the student's writing show little evidence of strategies tried?

- *Writing projects and plans.* Does the student's writing only reflect class units and work? Or does the writing show evidence of independent ideas and projects, such as fantasy stories, comics, or another untaught genre?

Finally, after observing the student and studying her work, you will want to have a conversation with her, perhaps ready to share some of your discoveries and theories with her. I find that it is often helpful to tell the student what I am conjecturing about. I might say something along the lines of, "Natalia, I noticed that you say, 'I'm done,' a lot during workshop time. I've been wondering why. Could I talk to you a little about what I'm thinking so far and maybe ask you some questions about your writing process?" Most students are flattered by the idea that we've been thinking about them. And, let's face it, most people enjoy the idea of talking about themselves. I also find that being honest with the students in turn encourages them to be honest with me. Here are a few questions you might ask during the conversation:

- When we have writing time, how do you feel about the amount of time we have? Too long? Too short? Just right?

- How do you know you're done?

- What do you normally do after you feel finished in writing when I am not available to ask what to do next?

- What plans do you have for your writing? Are there projects that you are working on or want to be working on?

The answers to these questions will help you determine how much of the student's declaration of being done comes from a place of actually feeling done and how much comes from simply not knowing what is possible to do next. It will also allow you to see if the writer has any aspirations that you can later mine while trying to support the student.

Strategies for Helping Students Who Declare Themselves Done

The first thing you need to do before moving on to actively teaching the student is to study your own perceptions of what it means to be done. Are you looking for a certain end product?

Are you hoping for a particular page count? Knowing what you would find acceptable as done will go a long way toward helping you decide which of the following strategies will work best for both you and the students.

For Students Who Are Looking for the Feeling of Being Finished

Almost every teacher I've ever met has a terrible secret that she shares only with her closest colleagues, and even then, often in hushed tones. Sometimes, on the last day of school, after all the students have headed off to their summer vacations, we find a stack of papers that we never graded. We wince. It is just more proof that we could never finish everything there was to finish. Even when the year is over and done. There is always just one more thing to do.

When thinking about the student who, quite simply, longs to just feel done, we can then start from a place of understanding.

Perhaps the best way to help a student who needs to know that something is at last completed is to help him create way stations inside the writing process—places where the writer can stop, admire the view, and catch his breath before moving on. Here are a few of the places that I suggest as natural stopping points for writers:

- after writing a particularly artful sentence or paragraph
- at the end of an entry in the notebook
- after a certain word count is met

- when an idea for a piece is chosen
- when a draft is finished
- when the first run of revisions is through

I find it is helpful to have a discussion with the writer about what would make a good stopping place for a mini-celebration of what has already been accomplished. The student can then jot down that way station on a sticky note and place it someplace visible so he knows that the time for celebration is near. Some writers will need to set several places to stop and take stock. Other writers will need to repeat the exercise only once or twice until they find their own stopping and starting rhythm.

For Students Who Have Not Yet Understood That Writing Is a Process

Despite the fact that we hang charts on our bulletin boards that outline the writing process (some of us even have clothespins with each student's name that the students can move as they go through the process) and lessons that are planned to follow process writing, many of us still come face-to-face with students who do not see writing as a process. They see it as a means to an end. And the sooner they get to that end, the better.

I believe that before we address the student who is struggling with process, it is important to reflect on our own teaching practices around process. Are we perhaps giving mixed messages on the value of product versus process? You might want to ask yourself a few of the following questions:

- Are my units all centered on genre? Or do I have a couple that have something to do with craft or process, such as a revision study or mentor authors?

- During share time, do I mostly have students share their day's triumphs? Or do I sometimes have students discuss their struggles and how they overcame them?

- Do I often talk and read about professional authors' processes? Or do I only read aloud great examples of literature without discussing theories about how they were made?

- Do I spend more time on editing for publication and making pieces presentable for publication than any other step of the process?

- When I give grades for writing, do I take into account the entire process the student followed? Or do I look at the final piece and grade only that?

Once you've answered those questions, you might find that some of the disconnect around process could be easily remedied with just a tweak or two in your own practice. Additionally, you might consider trying any of the following, with either your whole class or a few students:

- Create a "Process" bulletin board, where you hang the most interesting examples of writing process from students who are reveling in not being done.

- Offer different supplies to use at different steps of the writing process. Have strips of paper, tape, scissors, and highlighters available for revision. Have spell-checkers, editing pens, and grammar books available for editing.

▶ Collect stories of professional writers and their writing processes. Point out how different each writer is.

▶ Ask students to write or talk with a partner about their individual writing processes. Point out that some writers spend longer on some stages of the process than others. Everyone is different.

For Students Who Do Not Have a Purpose to Their Writing

There are as many different reasons that writers write as there are writers. Some writers write for love. Some for money. Others write because they have an audience in mind. Others because they have a topic they are passionate about. Still others write because they want to change the world.

Every writer needs to have a reason to write.

That said, we know that many of our students write simply because they are in school and we have asked them to. While this may help a student get something down on paper, it will not lead to the most inspired writing, nor will it solve the compulsion to just be done already. In order for a writer to want to linger on a piece, to take it through its paces and make it into the best work it can possibly be, he needs to have a purpose for writing it.

One of the ways we can ensure students have a purpose is by nurturing writing passions. Whether it be a genre or a topic of interest, we should work to connect each writer's passion with the piece she is currently working on. For example, if a student loves fantasy, perhaps she can write a literary essay about a fantasy novel and a poem with fantastical elements. If a student loves basketball, rather than coaching him to write about something else for the sake of variety, we can encourage him to embrace basketball as a life topic and explore it from every angle.

We can also work to develop an audience for the writing (parents, friends, first-grade reading buddies) and make sure the finished piece gets into the hands of that audience. If it's a bedtime story, it should be read aloud to a little one. If it's a letter, it should be mailed. If it's an op-ed, it should appear in a class newspaper.

Additionally, we can publish in compelling ways. Every writer loves to see her name in print. Some teachers type up class anthologies. Others offer bare books, blank hardcover books that students can fill up with their own writing and illustrations creating, in effect, their own hardcover books. A colleague of mine had her students create T-shirts with their poetry ironed onto them. Not every piece needs to have a big send-off, but by that same token, not every piece should be published on loose-leaf paper and hung on the bulletin board, either.

Your Reflections

As you come to end of this book, you might be feeling a little of the "I'm done" disease yourself. It's perhaps the most satisfying thing to say inside or outside of writing workshop. And yet it can wreak havoc in our classrooms.

Take a couple of minutes to jot down the names o[f]
dents in your class whom you have heard say, "I'm d[one]."

Then jot down your plans for next steps in worki[ng]
each of these students. Have you already interviewed and observed the student or do you still need to do that? What are
you already doing to support this student in developing his
own writing process? Have you made process a central com-
ponent in your teaching of writing? Or is that something you
might want to revisit, whether through explicit instruction,
studying a mentor author, or simply discussing your own
process?

One June, I wound my way around the classroom, conferring and observing and reading over students' shoulders, feeling pretty satisfied with just how productive my students had
become. Not one student appeared to be struggling. Everyone's head was bent to the task of writing. Then, all at once, my
idyllic tableau was shattered.

"I'm done!" Evanna proclaimed, a smile stretching across
her face.

I had to resist the urge to gasp out loud or turn and walk
away to catch my breath and regroup. Instead I did my best to
smile back. "Really?" I asked, almost teasingly.

"Nope. Not really," Evanna chirped and turned her smil-
ing face back toward her paper, where there was still a lot of
important work to be done.

WORKS CITED

Bender, J. 2007. *The Resourceful Writing Teacher: A Handbook of Essential Skills and Strategies*. Portsmouth, NH: Heinemann.

Bernays, A., and P. Painter. 2003. *What If?: Writing Exercises for Fiction Writers*. Upper Saddle River, NJ: Longman.

Burroway, J. 2006. *Imaginative Writing: The Elements of Craft*. Upper Saddle River, NJ: Longman.

Calkins, L. 1990. *Living Between the Lines*. Portsmouth, NH: Heinemann.

Cruz, M. C. 2004. *Independent Writing: One Teacher—Thirty-Two Needs, Topics, and Plans*. Portsmouth, NH: Heinemann.

Davis, J., and S. Hill. 2003. *The No-Nonsense Guide to Teaching Writing: Strategies, Structures, and Solutions*. Portsmouth, NH: Heinemann.

DiCamillo, K. n.d. "Scholastic: Teaching Resources." http://teacher.scholastic.com/activities/flashlightreaders/wd_blurb.htm.

Fletcher, R. 2006. *Boy Writers: Reclaiming Their Voices*. Portland, ME: Stenhouse.

Fletcher, R., and J. Portalupi. 2007. *Craft Lessons: Teaching Writing K–8*, Second Edition. Portland, ME: Stenhouse.

Graham, P. 1999. *Speaking of Journals: Children's Book Writers Talk About Their Diaries, Notebooks, and Sketchbooks*. Honesdale, PA: Boyds Mills Press.

Heard, G. 1998. *Awakening the Heart: Exploring Poetry in Elementary and Middle School*. Portsmouth, NH: Heinemann.

Janeczko, P. 2006. *Seeing the Blue Between: Advice and Inspiration for Young Poets*. Cambridge, MA: Candlewick.

Le Guin, U. 1998. *Steering the Craft: Exercises and Discussions on Story Writing for the Lone Navigator or the Mutinous Crew*. Portland, OR: The Eighth Mountain Press.

Lukeman, N. 2003. *The Plot Thickens: 8 Ways to Bring Fiction to Life*. New York: St. Martin's Griffin.

Ray, K. W. 2001. *The Writing Workshop: Working Through the Hard Parts (And They're All Hard Parts)*. Urbana, IL: National Council of Teachers of English.

Sciezska, J. n.d. "Reading Rockets: An Interview with Jon Sciezska." www.readingrockets.org/books/interviews/scieszka.

Snowball, D., and F. Bolton. 1999. *Spelling K–8: Planning and Teaching*. Portland, ME: Stenhouse.

Wilde, S. 2008. *Spelling Strategies and Patterns*. Portsmouth NH: *first*hand.

Woodson, Jacqueline. n.d. "Frequently Asked Questions." www.jacquelinewoodson.com/faq.shtml.

Zinsser, W. 2006. *On Writing Well: The Classic Guide to Writing Nonfiction*. London, UK: Collins.

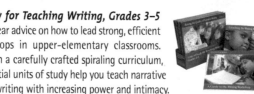